I0012216

Microsoft Powerpoint Guidebook

The Comprehensive Guide with Illustrations to master PowerPoint

By

Kai Torres

TABLE OF CONTENTS

CHAPTER 1: GETTING STARTED WITH POWERPOINT

PowerPoint Presentations: An Introduction

Similar to a word-processing tool like Word, PowerPoint is more focused on making presentations than documents. The Kodak Carousel slide trays that your grandfather filled with 35mm photos of the time he brought the family to the Grand Canyon in 1965 are similar to those in a presentation. The primary distinction between the two is that with PowerPoint, you don't have to stress about taking all the slides out of the tray and figuring out how to arrange them again.

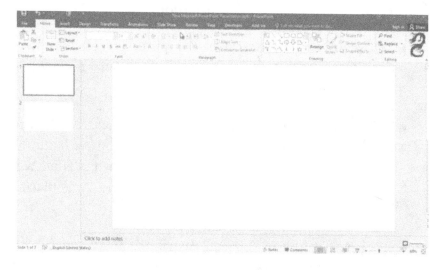

PowerPoint presentations include one or more slides, whereas Word documents have one or more pages. Each slide has the option to include text, images, animations, videos, and other types of content. A presentation's slides can be easily rearranged, unwanted slides can be removed, new slides can be added, and the content of current slides may be changed.

PowerPoint can be used to both produce presentations and deliver them.

To actually display your presentations, you can utilize a variety of media types, including:

- **Computer screen:** Your computer screen is a suitable way to display your presentation when you're showing it to just one or two other people.

- Big-screen TV: If you have a big-screen TV that can accommodate computer input, it's ideal for showing presentations to medium-size audiences — say, 10 to 12 people in a small conference room.

- **Computer projector:** A computer projector projects an image of your computer monitor onto a screen so large audiences can view it.

- **Videoconference screen share:** You can easily show your presentation by using the screen-sharing feature of your favorite videoconferencing platform. That way, your audience doesn't all have to be in the same place at the same time.

- **Printed pages:** You can distribute a printed copy of your entire presentation to each member of your audience. (When you print your presentation, you can print one slide per page, or you can print several slides per page to save paper.)

What's in a Slide?

One or more slides can be found in PowerPoint presentations. Text, images, and other items may be included on each slide. Several PowerPoint elements work together to make it simple for you to format eye-catching slides:

- **Slide layouts:** Every slide has a slide layout that determines how the information is displayed there. A slide layout is nothing more than a grouping of one or more placeholders that designate a space on the slide for the storage of data. The placeholders can contain text, graphics, clip art, sound or video files, tables, charts, graphs, diagrams, or other sorts of material, depending on the slide arrangement you select.

- **Background:** Every slide has a background, which serves as a stage for the information on the slide. The background can be a single color, a two-color gradient, a subtle texture like marble or parchment, a pattern like bricks, tiles, or diagonal lines, or even an image. Although each slide can have a different background, you should typically use the same background for each slide in your presentation to give it a uniform appearance.

- **Transitions:** When switching from one slide to the next, transitions regulate the visual effect that is used. It is customary for the following slide to replace the preceding slide without any splashy effects. However, you can choose to have one slide merge into the next, have new slides push older slides aside, or create the illusion that the previous slide has been removed by the wind in order to display the subsequent slide. There are about 50 transition effects in total that you may pick from.

- **Themes:** Themes are collections of design components that make it simple to generate engaging slides that don't appear tacky, like color schemes and fonts. You are free to deviate from the themes if you like, but you should only do so if your sense of design is superior to that of the Microsoft design experts.

- **Slide masters:** Slide masters are unique slides that regulate the fundamental formatting and design choices for the slides in your presentation. Slide masters and layouts are closely related; each layout includes a slide master that specifies the background and color scheme for the presentation, the typefaces, colors, and sizes of the fonts, as well as the location and size of the placeholders for the basic title and text. Additionally, you can include graphic and text items in slide masters that you want to present on each slide. To instantly modify the appearance of every slide in your presentation, edit the slide masters. This makes it easier to maintain the slides' uniform appearance.

In a similar manner that style sheets and templates control the design of Word documents, all the features mentioned in the list above work together to manage the appearance of your slides. Any of the features listed below can be added to individual slides to change their appearance:

- **Title and body text:** The majority of slide layouts provide spaces for the title and body content. Any text that you choose can be entered into these placeholders. PowerPoint styles the text by default in accordance with the slide master, but you may quickly change this formatting to use any font, size, style (such as bold or italic), or text color that you choose.

- **Text boxes:** By drawing a text box and then entering text, you can add text to any location on a slide. Text that doesn't fit neatly in the title or body text placeholders can be added using text boxes.

- **Shapes:** You may add a variety of shapes to your slides using the drawing tools in PowerPoint. The standard AutoShapes rectangles, circles, stars, arrows, and flowchart symbols are among the shapes that you can utilize. As an alternative, you can draw your own forms by hand or with simple line, polygon, and drawing tools.

- **Images:** You can add clip art, pictures, and other graphic elements to your slides to make them more visually appealing. Microsoft offers an even greater selection of clip art images online in addition to the extensive collection of images included with

PowerPoint. Of course, you can also insert images from your personal image library.

- **Charts and diagrams:** SmartArt, a slick diagramming function in PowerPoint, lets you make a variety of typical diagram kinds, such as organization charts and cycle diagrams. You can also include many additional chart kinds, such as pie charts, line charts, and bar charts.

- **Video and sound:** You can include audio or video elements in your slides. You can also include a personalized narration or background music.

- **Animations:** Animations move the numerous components on a single slide. One typical application of animation is to add movement to the text on the slide in order to draw the audience's attention. However, you can provide any slide's element motion.

Starting PowerPoint

Here's the procedure for starting PowerPoint:

1. **Get ready**

   Turn on a few votive candles. two Tylenol is taken. Get some coffee going. Take an allergy medication if you are allergic to banana slugs. Recite the Windows creed three times while seated in the lotus pose with Redmond, Washington, in your direction.

   My friend is Microsoft. It is pointless to resist. Homer becomes something when there is no alcohol or TV.

2. Your keyboard's Windows key should be depressed

The key with the elegant Windows flag printed on it is the Windows key. It is situated between the Alt and Tab keys on the majority of keyboards. The Start page, which displays when you click this button, displays a collection of your frequently used applications in huge tiles.

3. The PowerPoint tile can be selected by clicking it.

Simply put, that's how PowerPoint launches in a flash.

Another approach to launch PowerPoint is to tap the Windows key on your keyboard, which is typically located between the Ctrl and Alt keys. Then, simply type PowerPoint and press Enter.

Navigating the PowerPoint Interface

The items on this screen that are more crucial are highlighted in the list below:

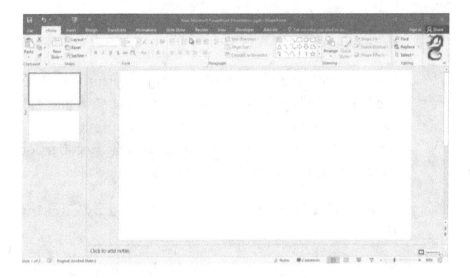

- **Ribbon:** The Ribbon is PowerPoint's primary user-interface tool, and it is located at the top of the screen, immediately beneath the Microsoft PowerPoint title. The Ribbon conceals PowerPoint's darkest and most sinister secrets. Whenever you explore it, wear a helmet.

  Depending on the size of your monitor, there are some little variations in the Ribbon's precise look. By utilizing smaller buttons and arranging them differently (for example, stacking them on top of one another instead of placing them side by side), PowerPoint may condense the Ribbon a little on smaller monitors.

- **File tab:** The File tab is the first item on the Ribbon. It puts PowerPoint in Backstage view so that you can carry out a variety of tasks like opening and saving files, making new presentations, printing, and other similar tasks.

- **Quick Access Toolbar:** Quick Access Toolbar or QAT for short, is located just above the Ribbon. Its main function is to give your most frequently used PowerPoint instructions a convenient resting spot.

  The QAT initially just had three commands: Save, Undo, and Redo. However, if you would like, you can add more commands. Right-click any button and select "Add to Quick Access Toolbar" to add it to the QAT. Additionally, a pull-down menu with a list of numerous frequently used commands can be found at the QAT's conclusion. These popular commands can be added to the QAT by using this menu.

- **Current slide**: Your current slide shows right in the center of the screen. (Take note that on a tablet, this slide's title section would read "Tap to Add Title" rather than "Click to Add Title.")

- **Slides pane:** An area that displays slide thumbnail icons is to the left of the slide. This section can be used to navigate quickly to other slides in your presentation.

- **Task pane**: The task pane is a section that is located to the right of the slide. The task pane is made to make it easier for you to finish routine chores quickly. The Design Ideas function in the task pane offers some design options for your bare presentation.

- **Status bar**: The status bar which is located at the very bottom of the screen, indicates which slide is presently being shown.

By right-clicking on the status bar, you can choose which elements appear there by selecting or deselecting from a selection of alternatives that appear.

- **Zoom control:** PowerPoint automatically adjusts the zoom level so that you can enlarge or reduce the size of your view of your slides. Using the zoom control slider that displays at the lower right of the window, you can modify the size of your slide.

If you believe that you must fully comprehend every dot on the PowerPoint screen before you can take any action, you will never accomplish anything. Concerning the things you don't understand, don't worry. Focus on the information you require to complete the task at hand; worry about the bells and whistles afterwards.

Unraveling the Ribbon

Microsoft's main user-interface tool is the Ribbon. A row of tabs runs horizontally across the top of the Ribbon. These tabs each have their own set of controls, which you can access by clicking one of them.

Additional tabs occasionally arise in addition to these fundamental tabs. For instance, if you pick an image, an image Tools menu with commands to edit the picture appears.

A Ribbon tab's commands are categorized into groups. Most of the actions within each group are straightforward buttons, much like the toolbar buttons in older versions of PowerPoint.

Editing Text

Slides in PowerPoint are empty spaces that you can decorate with various items. The most frequent object type is a text placeholder, which is a rectangular region created especially for holding text. Shapes like circles or triangles, images imported from clip art files, and graphs are examples of other object kinds.

The majority of presentations have two text objects: one for the title and one for the body text. However, you have the option to remove the body text and title text objects and add more text objects if you so choose. To make a slide without any text, you can even eliminate both.

The cursor transforms from an arrow to an I-beam whenever you move it over a text object, which can be used to construct aircraft carriers or support bridges. You can actually click the mouse and begin typing when the pointer turns into an I-beam.

A box surrounds the text when you click on a text object, and an insertion pointer appears where you clicked. Then, PowerPoint resembles a word processing program. Any characters you enter are placed where the insertion pointer is in the text. You can delete text by pressing Delete or Backspace, and you may move the insertion pointer inside a text object by using the arrow keys. A new line of text in the text object starts when you press the Enter key.

In the event that a text object is empty, a placeholder message is displayed. For instance, the message is displayed in a title text object. To add a title, click. Similar statements are displayed in other placeholders. When you click the object and start typing, the placeholder message mysteriously disappears.

The text you type is entered into the title text object if you begin typing without clicking anywhere, presuming the title text object does not already contain text. Any text you input (without selecting a text object) will be ignored if the title text object is not empty.

Press Esc or click anywhere outside the text object once you've finished typing.

To develop a blank presentation. Follow these steps:

1. On the title slide of the empty presentation, click anywhere in the placeholder text for "Click to Add Title."

2. Text to be typed is as follows: Let's Have a Thumb War!

That's accurate: You're going to make a straightforward PowerPoint presentation in this chapter that outlines the guidelines for the tra

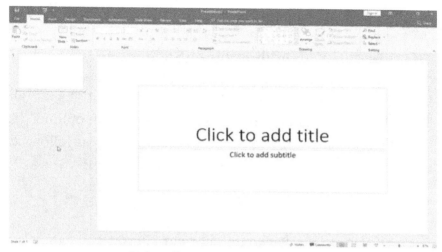

ditional game of thumb war.

3. Tap on anywhere in the Click to Add Subtitle placeholder.

4. Now input: The World's Least Barbaric Form of War.

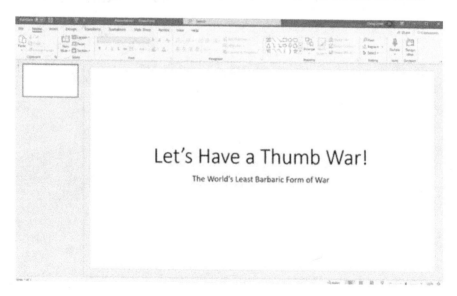

You're now done!

Adding a New Slide

One slide presentations aren't really presentations at all. Thankfully, PowerPoint offers you a variety of options for include more slides in your presentation. Let's go as follows to add a second slide to the Thumb War presentation:

1. **To insert a new slide, hit Ctrl+M.**

   If you have a keyboard shortcut allergy, you can select "New Slide" from the Home tab's list of options (in the margin).

   In either case, a fresh slide will show up.

2. Click anywhere within the Click to Add Title placeholder

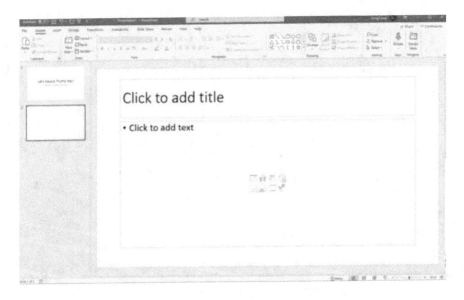

3. Click anywhere within the placeholder labeled "Click to Add Text," then enter each of the following words:

    1. Four-finger handshakes are exchanged.

    2. Chant "1, 2, 3, 4, Let's Have a Thumb War!" as you touch each other's index fingers with your thumbs in an alternating left-to-right motion.

    3. War is begun! Attempt to enclose your opponent's thumb in your own.

    4. You've won the thumb war if you can hold your opponent's thumb in place long enough to yell, "1, 2, 3, 4, I Won the Thumb War!"

Note that you don't have to enter the bullet symbols — PowerPoint automatically adds a new bulleted paragraph when you press the Enter key.

Moving from Slide to Slide

You need to understand how to advance and rewind through your presentation now that it has more than one slide. Here are a few of the most widely used techniques:

- At the base of the vertical scroll bar, select one of the double-headed arrows. You advance through the presentation one slide at a time by doing this.

- Page Up or Page Down must be selected. These keys also advance the slide one at a time.

- Employ the scroll bar. The number and title of the current slide are displayed in a tooltip when you drag the box in the scroll bar. The quickest way to navigate directly to any slide in your presentation is by dragging the scroll bar.

- Click the thumbnail of the slide you wish to display in the list of slides on the left side of the window. Click the Slides tab up top if you can't see the thumbnails.

Closing a Presentation

You're now ready to close your presentation after finishing and saving it. A presentation's conclusion is similar to gathering your materials, organizing them neatly in a file folder, then placing the file folder back in its rightful file drawer. You can no longer see the presentation on your computer screen. You can access it later if necessary because it is safely stored on your hard drive.

Click the Close button in the PowerPoint window's upper right corner to shut down a file. You can also use the keyboard shortcut Ctrl+W or click the File tab, then select Close. The simplest method to close a file is, however, to click the Close button.

Before leaving PowerPoint, a file does not need to be closed. PowerPoint kindly closes the file for you if you leave the program without doing so. The only occasion you might want to close a file is if you need to work on another file and don't want to have two windows open at once.

PowerPoint offers to save any modifications you've made since the previous time you saved the document. Before closing the document, you can save it by clicking Save, or you can choose not to save any changes you've made by clicking Don't Save.

The majority of the PowerPoint commands might no longer work if all open PowerPoint presentations are closed. (On the menu, they are grayed out.) Be at ease. The commands come back to life if you start a new presentation or open an existing one.

Getting Help

The most desirable approach to utilizing PowerPoint would involve having a knowledgeable PowerPoint expert at your side, patiently addressing your queries with clear responses, gently rectifying any trivial errors you make, and otherwise minding their own business. In this scenario, all you would need to do is occasionally offer the expert a Twinkie and allow them a daily break outside.

If such a scenario is not feasible, the next best option is to learn how to prompt PowerPoint itself to provide the answers you require. Fortunately, PowerPoint incorporates a helpful built-in feature known as Help, which can address your inquiries. No matter how deeply you find yourself entangled in the complexities of PowerPoint, assistance is always just a few clicks or keystrokes away.

Similar to other Office applications, multiple methods are available for accessing help when needed. The simplest approach would be to exclaim "Skipper!" in your best Gilligan voice. Alternatively, the following options are at your disposal:

- Press F1 or click the Help button located on the left edge of the Help tab in the Ribbon. This will activate PowerPoint's main Help system.

- Whenever a dialog box appears, you can click the question mark button in the upper-right corner to summon help.

- When you hover the mouse over an item in the Ribbon, a tooltip emerges, providing an explanation of its function. Many of these tooltips include the phrase "Press F1 for more help." In such cases, pressing F1 will provide help specific to that item.

The Help tab offers several means of accessing the assistance you require. Here are the various ways you can navigate PowerPoint's Help feature:

- **Help window links**: By clicking any of the links displayed in the Help tab, you can access help on specific topics. For instance, selecting "Pictures and Charts" will present you with a page containing useful information about working with images and charts.

- **Search**: If you are unable to locate what you need, you can try entering a word or phrase in the Search box and clicking the Search button. This will generate a list of topics related to the entered word or phrase.

- **Back button**: By utilizing the Help window's Back button, you can retrace your steps. You can repeatedly use the Back button to backtrack as far as necessary.

- **Home button**: This button returns you to the Help home page.

Other icons on the Help tab of the Ribbon enable you to contact Microsoft Support, provide feedback on PowerPoint features that please or frustrate you, explore training opportunities for quick PowerPoint learning, and discover new features.

CHAPTER 2: TAKING THE BACKSTAGE TOUR

Welcome to Backstage View

Backstage view has three main pages:

- **Home**: This option allows you to create a new presentation either from scratch or using a limited set of predefined themes and templates. It also provides quick access to recently used presentations.

- **New**: This option provides additional choices for creating presentations based on various themes and templates.

- **Open**: By selecting this option, you can access recently used presentations or search for other existing presentations on your computer or online.

If you already have a presentation open in PowerPoint, you can switch to Backstage view at any time by clicking on the File tab. This will display a slightly different version of Backstage view. Alongside the standard Home, New, and Open pages, this version of Backstage view offers additional options:

- **Info**: This page presents interesting details about the current presentation.

- **Save a Copy**: By selecting this option, you can create a duplicate of the current presentation with a different file name or in a different folder location.

- **Print**: This option enables you to print your presentation.

- **Share**: This option allows you to share your presentation with other individuals.

- **Export**: By choosing this option, you can save your presentation in an alternative format, such as a PDF file or a video file.

- **Close**: This option closes the currently active presentation.

Considering Themes and Templates

It can be difficult to start from scratch while making a presentation. Thankfully, PowerPoint has a huge library of themes and templates you may utilize to get going. What's the distinction between themes and templates? Glad you inquired:

- **Theme:** Colors, fonts, backgrounds, and other formatting options are all included in a theme's collection of formatting components. You can quickly make attractive presentations using themes. Additionally, you can quickly alter the theme if you aren't happy with the way your presentation appears.

- **Templates:** Templates serve as a combination of a theme and pre-existing content. They are specifically designed to assist you in initiating a particular type of presentation, such as a sales pitch, quarterly report, or design proposal. Unlike themes, applying a template to an existing presentation would overwrite your content with the content included in the template.

To create a new presentation using a theme or template, click on "New." This will open the New page.

At the top of the New page, you will find a selection of suggested themes and templates. If none of them suit your preferences, you can browse or search for the ideal theme or template from the extensive collection provided by PowerPoint.

To search for a theme or template, enter a search term in the Search box and press Enter or click the magnifying glass. Alternatively, you can select one of PowerPoint's suggested search categories, such as Presentations, Themes, Education, Charts, Diagrams, Business, or Infographics.

If you don't find anything suitable, you can click "Back" to return to the New page or refine your search by modifying the text in the Search box and pressing Enter.

If you come across a theme or template you like, follow these steps to create a presentation from it:

1. Click on the desired theme or template. This will open a window. Displaying various color variations for the theme.

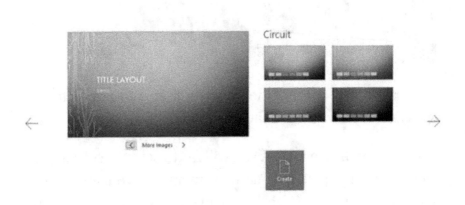

2. If you selected a theme, choose one of the available color variations for that theme. Note that this step is applicable only to themes, as templates do not offer color variations.

3. Optionally, use the "More Images" control to preview how different types of slides will appear with the selected theme or template. Click the ">" or "<" buttons to navigate through the available slide images. Please note

that for templates, using the "More Images" control will show you the slides that will be inserted into your presentation when you create the template. For themes, no slides will be inserted into the presentation.

4. Finally, click on "Create" (indicated in the margin) to generate the presentation based on the chosen theme or template.

If you wish to ensure that a specific theme or template appears in the list of suggestions at the top of the New pane, you can right-click on the respective theme or template and select "Pin to List." Conversely, to remove a theme or template from the list, right-click on it and choose "Remove from List."

Saving Your Presentation

To force a theme or template to appear in the list of suggestions at the top of the New pane, right-click on it and select "Pin to List." To remove a theme or template from the list, right-click on it and choose "Remove from List."

There are various options available when saving your presentation files:

- **Recent**: Enables you to choose from locations where you have recently stored presentation files.

- **OneDrive**: Allows you to save the file in your OneDrive storage.

- **This PC**: Lets you save the file to a specific location on your computer.

- **Add a Place**: Permits you to add other cloud locations for easy access.

- **Browse**: Enables you to directly browse to the desired save location.

Once you save a file for the first time, the name displayed in the presentation window's title area will change from "Presentation" to the name you have given to the file. This change confirms that the file has been successfully saved.

When choosing a name for a new file, it's important to use your creativity and select a meaningful name that reflects the content of the file. This will help you easily identify the file later on.

It's crucial not to work on a file for long periods without saving it. It is recommended to save your work every few minutes to avoid any potential loss of data. Unexpected events like power outages or computer malfunctions can occur, so developing a habit of frequent saving is essential. Remember to save your presentation after making significant changes, such as adding multiple new slides or making complex formatting modifications.

The following sections provide step-by-step instructions on how to save your file on your computer and in OneDrive, as well as how to create a copy of your presentation.

Saving to a location on your computer

To save a new file to a specific location on your computer, follow these steps:

1. Switch to Backstage view by selecting the File tab. You will be directed to the Save As page in Backstage view. Then choose Save.

2. Click on Browse.

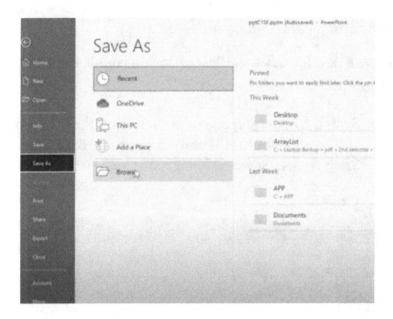

The Save As dialog box will appear.

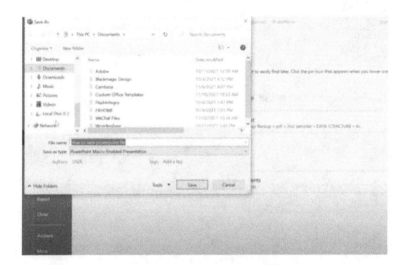

3. Navigate to the folder where you want to save the file. If needed, create a new folder for the file by clicking on New Folder.

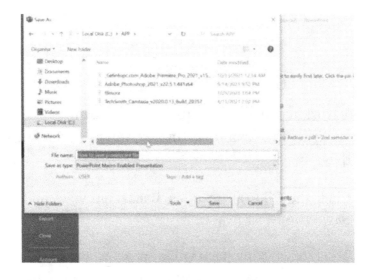

4. Modify the filename if the proposed one is not suitable.

5. Click Save.

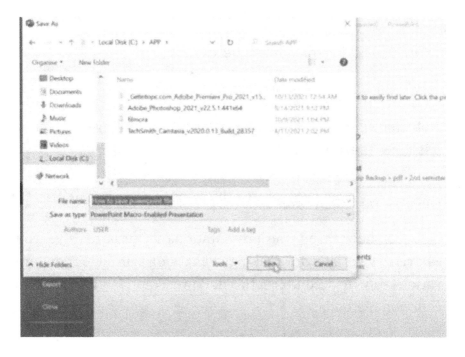

Congratulations! Your file is now saved.

Saving a copy of a presentation

If you're working on a presentation and decide to save a copy of it with a different filename or in a different folder (or both), follow these steps:

1. Click the File tab to open Backstage view and choose Save a Copy.

2. The Save a Copy page will appear, which is identical to the Save As page when saving a presentation for the first time.

3. Navigate to the desired location where you want to save the file.

4. Modify the filename if necessary.

5. Click Save to create your copy.

Note that when you save a copy, you will be working on the copy itself, not the original file.

Opening a Presentation

Once you have saved your presentation to your hard drive, you can retrieve it later for making changes or printing. There are various ways to accomplish this in PowerPoint, but here are two common methods:

- Click the File tab to switch to Backstage view and choose Open.

- Alternatively, press Ctrl+O.

Both options will take you to the Open screen in Backstage view. From here, you can select a file from the list of recently opened presentations or open a file saved in your OneDrive account.

To browse your computer for a file, click the Browse icon. This will bring up the Open dialog box, which allows you to navigate through different folders on your hard drive to locate your files. If you know how to open a file in any Windows application, you will be familiar with this process in PowerPoint since the Open dialog box is similar across Windows programs.

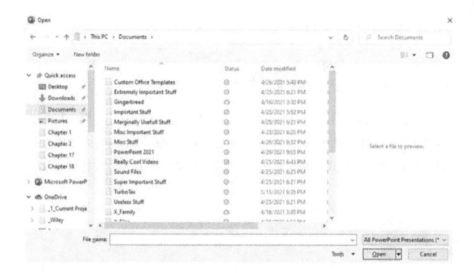

If you can't find a file, try searching in different folders. It's possible that you accidentally saved it in the wrong folder. Also, check the filename for any spelling errors. Sometimes, mistyping the filename can result in difficulties finding the file.

Tip: The fastest way to open a file from the Open dialog box is to double-click it. This saves you from having to click the file once and then click OK. Double-clicking also helps exercise the fast-twitch muscles in your index finger.

CHAPTER 3: EDITING SLIDES

Moving from Slide to Slide

To navigate through a PowerPoint presentation on a computer, you have several options:

- **Page Down:** Press the Page Down key to move forward to the next slide.

- **Page Up:** Press the Page Up key to move backward to the previous slide.

To move around in your presentation, you can also utilize the vertical scroll bar on the right side of the window:

- **Double-headed arrows:** Click the double-headed arrows at the bottom of the vertical scroll bar to move one slide forward or backward at a time.

- **Single-headed arrows:** Click and hold the single-headed arrow at the top or bottom of the vertical scroll bar to scroll continuously forward or backward through the presentation. Note that if the zoom level allows only one slide to be visible, clicking the single-headed arrows moves to the next or previous slide.

- **Scroll box:** Drag the scroll bar up or down to quickly move between slides. A tooltip will appear next to the scroll bar, indicating which slide will be displayed when you release the mouse.

If you have a touchscreen device, you can use a finger flick to move from slide to slide.

These methods provide different ways to navigate through your PowerPoint presentation, allowing you to choose the one that suits you best.

Working with Objects

MoMost of the elements on your slides are text objects, which allow you to enter and display text on your slides.

Each slide has a predefined layout that includes one or more designated areas called placeholders. A placeholder is a reserved space on a slide for adding text, clip art, graphs, or other types of objects. For instance, a slide using the Title layout typically has two text placeholders—one for the title and another for the subtitle. You can choose the slide layout and placeholders when creating new slides using the Slide Layout task pane. Later on, you can modify the layout, add more objects, delete, move, or resize them as needed.

You have the option to add various types of objects to your slides, such as clip art, charts, graphs, shapes, and more. There are different tools available on the Drawing toolbar located at the bottom of the screen, as well as icons in the center of slides created using Content layouts, to assist you in adding objects to your slides.

Each object occupies a rectangular area on the slide. The content within the object may or may not fully fill the rectangular space, but the outline of the object becomes visible when selected.

It is possible for objects to overlap. Typically, you would aim to avoid overlapping objects, but in some cases, doing so can create an interesting visual effect. For example, you might want to place text on top of clip art for a more visually appealing composition.

Selecting objects

You must first choose the object that includes the text, image, or other element that you want to alter on a slide. For instance, editing text onscreen cannot be done by just starting to type. The text object containing the text you wish to change must first be chosen. To change the contents of other types of objects, you must choose them first.

You must be in Normal view in order to pick certain slide items. You can choose entire slides in the Slide Sorter view, but not their individual components.

The following principles should be kept in mind when choosing objects:

- **Text objects**: Move the insertion point over the text you wish to edit, then click, to choose the text object and edit it. (Double-tap the text on a touchpad.) You can begin typing after a text insertion point and a rectangle box surround the object.

- **Non-text objects**: Other object kinds function somewhat differently. When you click an object, it is selected. To let you know that you've hooked something, a rectangle box appears all around the object. After hooking an item, you can move it across the screen or alter its size, but you can't change what's inside of it.

- **The Ctrl key:** Using the Ctrl key, you can pick several items by clicking the first item, then selecting additional items while continuing to hold down the Ctrl key.

- **Click and drag:** You may also use the insertion point to drag a rectangle around the items you wish to pick in order to select one or more of them. Click and drag the mouse down and to the right until a rectangle encloses the object(s) you wish to pick from a location above and to the right of it. All of the objects inside the rectangle are chosen when the button is released.

- **The Tab key**: To pick things, press the Tab key on your keyboard. To choose the very first slide object, press Tab once. To choose the following object, press Tab once more. Tab repeatedly until the desired object is selected.

When you can't readily point to the thing you want to choose, using Tab to select it is useful. This issue can arise if the item you want is hidden beneath another object, is empty, or is otherwise invisible and you are unsure of its location.

Resizing or moving an object

When an object is selected, a box appears around it. This box has handles called "love handles" located on each corner and the middle of each edge. These love handles can be used to adjust the size of the object. Additionally, you can grab the edge of the box between the love handles to move the object on the slide. These handles are technically referred to as "sizing handles."

When you move or resize an object, it tends to align itself with nearby objects. Alignment lines will appear when you move the object into alignment with other objects on the slide. If you release the mouse button when the alignment marks appear, the object will snap into place according to the indicated alignment.

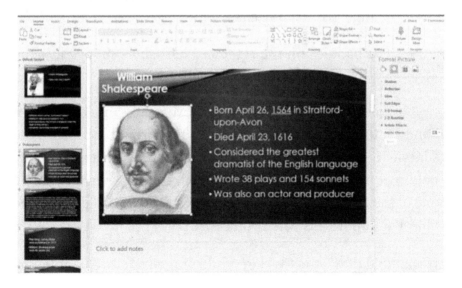

Certain objects, such as shapes and graphics, may have a circular arrow known as the "rotate handle" floating above them. You can rotate the object by grabbing this handle and dragging it in a circular motion. However, not all objects can be rotated, such as charts.

To change the size of an object, select the object and then click and hold one of the love handles. While holding down the mouse button, move the mouse to adjust the object's size.

The various handles on an object provide different ways to change its size:

- The handles at the corners enable you to change both the height and the width of the object.

- The handles on the top and bottom edges enable you to change just the object's height.

- The handles on the right and left edges change just the width of the object.

If you hold down the Ctrl key while you drag one of the love handles, the object stays centered at its current position on the slide as its size adjusts. Try it to see what I mean. Also, try holding down the Shift key while you drag an object by using one of the corner love handles. This combination maintains the object's proportions when you resize it.

If you hold down the Ctrl key while dragging a love handle, the object will remain centered at its current position on the slide as its size is adjusted. You can try this to see the effect.

Additionally, holding down the Shift key while dragging a corner love handle maintains the object's proportions during resizing.

Changing the size of a text object doesn't affect the size of the text itself; it only adjusts the size of the frame containing the text. Changing the width of a text object is similar to adjusting margins in a word-processing program, as it widens or narrows the text lines. To resize the text within a text object, you need to change the font size.

To move an object, click anywhere on the outline box, except on a love handle, and then drag the object to its new position. For shapes and graphics, you can click and drag anywhere within the object to move it. However, for objects containing text, you must click on the outline box itself to move the object to a new location.

The outline box might be difficult to see if you have a visually busy background on your slides. If you experience trouble seeing the outline box when selecting an object, you can try squinting or cleaning your monitor screen. Alternatively, you can go to the View tab on the Ribbon and choose one of the Color/Grayscale options:

- **Color**: Displays slides in full color

- **Grayscale**: Displays colors as shades of gray

- **Pure Black and White**: Displays the slides in black and white

Viewing the slide in Grayscale or Pure Black and White might make the love handles easier to spot. To switch back to full-color view, click Back to Color View.

Editing a Text Object

When you choose a text object to edit in PowerPoint, the software transforms into a simplified word processor, enabling text modification. It's important to note that PowerPoint automatically wraps text, eliminating the need to press Enter at the end of each line, except when you want to start a new paragraph.

In PowerPoint presentations, paragraphs are typically formatted with a bullet character at the beginning. The specific bullet character used depends on the applied theme. However, if you're unsatisfied with the default bullet provided by the theme, you have the flexibility to customize it with various shapes. Remember that the bullet character is a part of the paragraph format and doesn't require manual typing within the text.

To navigate within a text object, you can use the arrow keys or the mouse. The End and Home keys are also available to move the insertion point to the start or end of the current line. For quicker navigation, combining the arrow keys with the Ctrl key allows for faster movement. For example, pressing Ctrl along with the left or right arrow key moves the insertion point an entire word at a time.

Deleting text is as simple as using the Delete or Backspace keys. To delete from the insertion point to the start or end of a word, the Ctrl key can be used in conjunction with the Delete or Backspace key. If you select a block of text before pressing Delete or Backspace, the entire selection will be deleted. (The next section provides tips on selecting text.)

Selecting Text

Some text-editing operations — such as amputations and transplants — require that you first select the text on which you want to operate. Here's how to select blocks of text:

- When using the keyboard, hold down the Shift key while you press any of the arrow keys to move the insertion point.

- When using the mouse, point to the beginning of the text that you want to mark and then click and drag over the text. Release the mouse button when you reach the end of the text that you want to select.

PowerPoint has an automatic word-selection option that tries to guess when you intend to select an entire word. If you use the mouse to select a block of text that spans the space between two words, the selected text jumps to include entire words while you move the mouse. If you don't like this feature, you can disable it by clicking the File tab and then the Options button in Backstage view. Then deselect the When Selecting, Automatically Select Entire Word check box.

You can use the following tricks to select different amounts of text:

- **A single word:** To select a single word, point the insertion point anywhere in the word and double-click.

- **An entire paragraph:** To select an entire paragraph, point the insertion point anywhere in the paragraph and triple-click. (Although this works with a mouse, you can't select an entire paragraph by triple-tapping on a touchscreen.)

After you've selected text, you can edit it in the following ways:

- **Delete**: To delete the entire block of text that you've selected, press Delete or Backspace.

- **Replace**: To replace an entire block of text, select it and then begin typing. The selected block vanishes and is replaced by the text that you're typing.

- **Cut, Copy, and Paste**: You can use the Cut, Copy, and Paste commands from the Clipboard group with selected text blocks. The following section describes these commands.

Using Cut, Copy, and Paste

PowerPoint, like other Windows programs, utilizes the familiar Cut, Copy, and Paste commands. These commands can be applied to selected text or entire objects. In simpler terms, you can use Cut, Copy, and Paste for both portions of text and whole objects.

These commands interact with the Clipboard, a mysterious feature of Windows that stores items for later use. When you execute Cut or Copy, the selected content is added to the Clipboard, and the Paste command retrieves and inserts the content into your presentation.

For basic cutting, copying, and pasting, you can rely on the standard Windows keyboard shortcuts: Ctrl+X for Cut, Ctrl+C for Copy, and Ctrl+V for Paste. Since these shortcuts work across most Windows programs, memorizing them is advantageous.

The Ribbon buttons responsible for Clipboard actions are located in the Clipboard group of the Home tab. This section contains four buttons, three of which are relevant to Clipboard operations:

It's worth noting that the Copy button includes a drop-down arrow. Clicking the Copy icon itself copies the selected object to the Clipboard. However, if you click the drop-down arrow, a small menu with two icons appears. The first icon copies the selection, while the second creates a duplicate. More information on duplicating an object can be found in the next section, "Duplicating an Object."

An interesting feature of PowerPoint allows you to preview the contents of the Clipboard before pasting them into your slide. To utilize this feature, copy or cut something to the Clipboard, then click the downward arrow beneath the Paste button. This action reveals a menu with various paste options represented by buttons. By hovering over each button, you can preview how the item will appear when pasted. Once you find the desired paste preview, click the corresponding button to perform the paste.

If you want to permanently remove an entire object, select it and press the Delete or Backspace key. This action deletes the object from the slide without copying it to the Clipboard. It is irretrievable, except through the Undo command, which should be used promptly.

It's important to note that PowerPoint allows you to paste text copied from external sources such as Word or Excel. When using the Paste button or the Ctrl+V shortcut, the pasted text assumes the formatting of the PowerPoint text it is inserted into. However, if you wish to retain the original formatting from the Word or Excel document, you can right-click the insertion point, select Paste Options, and choose to keep the source formatting or adopt the destination formatting. Additionally, you have the option to insert the copied text as a picture, which preserves its appearance but renders it uneditable.

To include the same object on every slide consistently, there's a more efficient method than copying and pasting: add the object to the slide master, which governs the format of all slides in a presentation.

Using the Clipboard Task Pane

Using the Clipboard task window, you can choose to paste up to 24 bits of text or graphics from any Office product into your presentation. To open the Clipboard task pane, click the dialog box launcher on the Ribbon's Home tab, which is located in the bottom right corner of the Clipboard group. The Clipboard task pane is located on the left side of the PowerPoint window and currently contains several elements.

To copy something from the task pane to the clipboard, just click the thing you want to put.

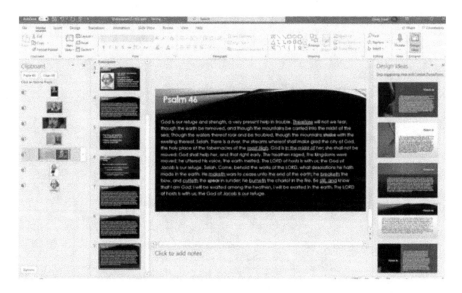

Working with Slide Layouts

In PowerPoint, the arrangement of various object placeholders on a slide is referred to as the slide layout. The Title Slide layout and the Title and Content layout are the two slide layout types that we have mostly used in this book. However, there are a lot more layout possibilities in PowerPoint.

A new slide is automatically set to the Text with Content layout when you insert it. Click the down arrow next to the New Slide icon (in the margin) if you wish to introduce a slide with a different layout. This will reveal a drop-down gallery with all of the slide arrangement options. To apply the required layout to the new slide, just choose it from the gallery.

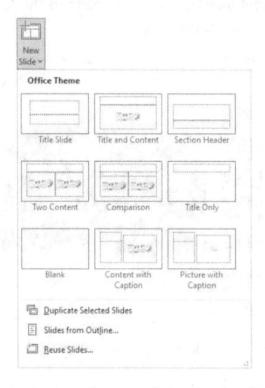

When you use a theme in your presentation, the gallery will display the slide designs that go along with it.

Use the Layout button (visible in the margin) in the Slides section of the Home tab to modify the layout of an existing slide. To begin editing a slide, select it and then click the Layout option. You'll see a gallery with a number of layout choices. The layout you select from the gallery will be applied to the chosen slide.

Deleting a Slide

Do you wish to remove a complete slide? No issue. Simply move your cursor over the slide you wish to remove, then click the Delete button located in the Slides group of the Home tab's Ribbon. Zowie! The slide is old news.

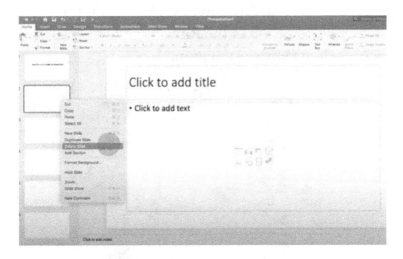

A slide can also be deleted by clicking its thumbnail in the Slide Preview window (on the left side of the screen), followed by the Delete or Backspace keys.

If you accidentally deleted the wrong slide, no issue. To restore the slide, simply hit Ctrl+Z or click the Undo option.

Duplicating a Slide

You can duplicate a whole slide in PowerPoint, including the text, styling, and other features, by using the Duplicate Slide command. As a result, after spending hours polishing a slide's layout, you can make a copy of it to use as the model for another slide.

To duplicate a slide or slides, select the slide(s) you want to duplicate. Then, pick the Duplicate Selected Slides button by clicking the arrow next to the Add Slide button in the Slides group on the Home tab of the Ribbon. You duplicate the slide and include it in your presentation.

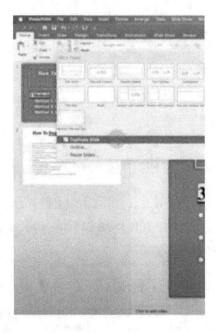

If you're a keyboard shortcut addict, just choose the slide you want to duplicate in the Slides pane (located on the left side of the screen) and press Ctrl+D.

Replacing Text

Let's imagine that the Rent-a-Nerd business decides to enter the sports consulting industry and wants to rebrand as Rent-a-Jock. Easy. Simply use the handy Replace command to change every instance of "Nerd" to "Jock". The following are the steps:

1. The Replace button in the Editing group on the Home tab of the Ribbon can be accessed by pressing the keyboard shortcut Ctrl+H. It is visible in the margin.

2. In the Find What box, type the text you're looking for.

    Type the text you want to change (in this case, "nerd") into the appropriate field.

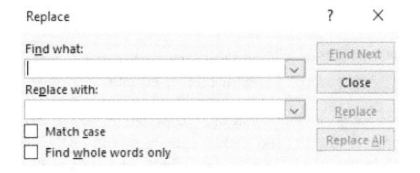

3. Enter the replacement text in the Replace With box.

    Put the text you want to use to change what you entered (in this case, Jock) in the Find What box.

4. Choose Next under Find.

The first instance of the text is located using PowerPoint.

5. Click the Replace option to alter the text.

Read the material first to be sure it found what you were looking for.

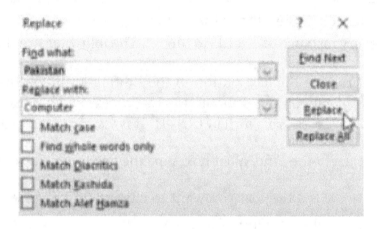

6. Repeat the Find Next and Replace process until it is finished.

Click Find Next to locate the next instance, replace it, and so forth. Continue till the very end.

If you are positive that you want to swap out every occurrence of your Find What text with the Replace With text, click the Replace All button. In this stage, the Find Next and Replace cycle is omitted. The only drawback is that the replacement will invariably be unwelcome in at least one area. For instance, Sglovey instead of Smitty results from changing the word "mitt" to "glove." Keep in mind that you may also use the Find Whole

Words Only option to find and replace text only if it appears as a whole word.

You can utilize the Undo option to restore your presentation to its original state if you choose Replace All and completely muck it up.

Rearranging Your Slides in Slide Sorter View

You normally change your slides, rearrange objects, add text or images, and perform other activities using the conventional view. Normal view, on the other hand, has a huge disadvantage in that it does not provide you a full picture of your presentation. Only a few slides can be seen in the Slide Preview box, and only one slide can be displayed in detail at time. For a complete view of your presentation, use the Slide Sorter view.

There are two simple ways to change to the Slide Sorter view:

- Select the Slide Sorter button located on the right side of the status bar.

- After selecting the View tab on the Ribbon, click the Slide Sorter button in the Presentation Views group.

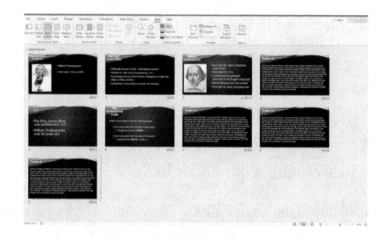

The techniques listed below can be used to arrange, add, or remove slides from the Slide Sorter view:

- **Move a slide:** Slides can be moved simply clicking on them and dragging them to a new location. While aiming at the slide, keep the mouse button depressed. After dragging the slide to its new location, let go of the button. The presentation is altered by PowerPoint to reflect the new slide order.

- **Delete a slide:** Click the slide to select it, then press the Delete or Backspace key to remove it. This is only supported by the Slide Sorter view.

- **Add a new slide:** Click the slide you want the new slide to follow, then click the New Slide button to add a new slide. You may choose the layout for the new slide by opening the Slide Layout task pane. Return to Normal view using the view buttons in the Status bar, the View tab on the Ribbon, or by double-clicking the brand-new slide to edit the slide's content.

The Slide Sorter view is where you can add fantastic animation effects, build effects, and jazzy transitions to your slides, despite the fact that it could seem dull and uninteresting. For instance, you can make your bullets fall from the top of the screen like explosives and switch between slides by using strips, wipes, or blinds.

CHAPTER 4: WORKING IN OUTLINE VIEW

Calling Up the Outline

When in Normal view, the left side of the PowerPoint window is used to show thumbnails of your presentations. However, you can rapidly switch your presentation to outline mode by simply pressing the Outline mode button (shown in the margin) on the Ribbon's View tab. The titles of each slide appear as independent headings at the top level of the outline, with the content on each slide displaying as lower-level headings behind the slide headers. If a slide doesn't have a title, the top-level heading is blank, but it still appears in the outline.

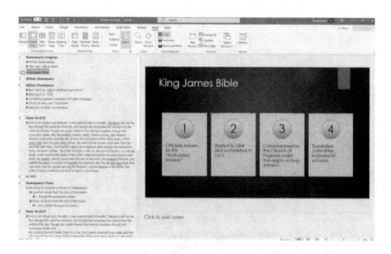

You can enlarge the area set aside for the outline by clicking and dragging the Outline window's boundary.

The following list highlights a few crucial points from the outline:

- **The outline contains the headings and body text for each slide.** Anything else you include on a slide, such as pictures, graphs, and so on, is not included in the outline. Additionally, any text objects that you add to the slide in addition to the placeholders for the title and body content will not be included in the outline.

- **Each slide has a high-level heading in the outline.** The text of this heading is taken from the slide's title, and an icon unique to that slide is shown next to it. The slide number is also located to the left of the Slide sign.

- **Each text line from a slide's body text is shown with an indented header.** This heading appears beneath the slide's main title heading.

- **An outline can incorporate the subpoints that follow the main points on each slide.** Up to nine heading levels can be added to each presentation in PowerPoint, although more than two heading levels will probably make your slides too complicated.

Selecting and Editing an Entire Slide

The Outline tab often requires you to choose an entire slide in order to interact with it. This can be done by selecting the slide's icon, which automatically selects the slide's title, body text, and any other objects like graphics, even if they are not visible in the outline.

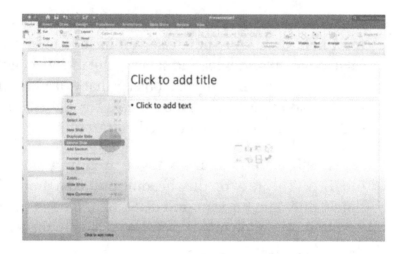

You have several options for managing entire slides in PowerPoint:

- **Delete**: To remove a whole slide, select it and press the Delete key.

- **Cut or copy**: To cut or copy an entire slide to the Clipboard, select the slide and use Ctrl+X (Cut) or Ctrl+C (Copy) keyboard shortcuts. Alternatively, you can use the Cut or Copy button on the Home tab of the Ribbon. Once the slide is cut or copied, you can navigate to any location in the outline and press Ctrl+V or use the Paste button to insert the slide from the Clipboard. Another way to cut or copy a slide is by right-clicking the slide and choosing Cut or Copy from the menu.

- **Duplicate**: To create a copy of a slide, select it and press Ctrl+D. This action duplicates the selected slide and places the copy immediately after it. It's not necessary to select the entire slide for duplication; simply clicking anywhere in the slide's title or body text is enough.

Selecting and Editing One Paragraph

To work with paragraphs and their hierarchy in PowerPoint, you can use the following actions:

- **Selecting and deleting**: To select an entire paragraph along with its subordinate paragraphs, click the bullet next to the desired paragraph. Press the Delete key to delete the selected paragraph and its subordinates.

- **Cut or copy**: To cut or copy an entire paragraph, including its subordinates, select it and use Ctrl+X (Cut) or Ctrl+C (Copy) keyboard shortcuts. You can then use Ctrl+V to paste the paragraph anywhere in the presentation.

Moving Text Up and Down

It's easy to rearrange your presentation using the outline. The sequence of the slides can be easily changed, as can the order of the individual points on a slide.

By right-clicking the paragraphs you want to shift and selecting the appropriate option from the pop-up menu, you may rearrange your presentation. A bullet adjacent to the paragraph you want to move can also be pointed out. Once the four-cornered arrow cursor appears, click and drag the text up or down. The selection's horizontal location is indicated by a horizontal line that appears. When the horizontal line is where you want the text to be, release the mouse button.

When repositioning text in a slide with multiple levels of body text paragraphs, take caution. When you move the selection, pay attention to where the horizontal line appears; the complete selection is inserted there, possibly dividing up subpoints. You can always undo a move if you don't like the outcome by using Ctrl+Z or the Undo button.

CHAPTER 5: CREATING GOOD LOOKING SLIDES

Exploring the Many Types of Pictures

The world is awash with many different picture file formats. Fortunately, PowerPoint works with almost all these formats. The following sections describe the two basic types of pictures you can work with in PowerPoint: bitmap pictures and vector drawings.

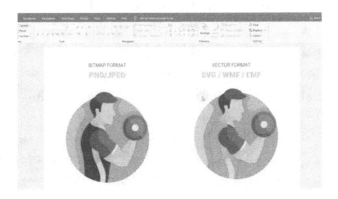

Bitmap pictures

A bitmap picture is formed by a collection of small dots that come together to create a picture. These pictures are commonly used for photographs as well as icons and buttons on websites. To create bitmap images, you can utilize tools like a scanner, a digital camera, or software like Adobe Photoshop. Even Microsoft Paint, which comes free with Windows, can be used to create basic bitmap images.

The dots that form a bitmap image are known as pixels. The number of pixels in an image determines its resolution, which is stated in terms of width and height. For instance, an image that is 1,000 pixels wide and 600 pixels tall has a resolution of 1,000 x 600 pixels.

To calculate the total number of pixels in an image, you multiply the width by the height. Therefore, a 1,000 x 600 pixel image would have a total of 600,000 pixels.

Pixel density refers to the number of pixels per inch when displaying or printing an image. For example, if a 1,000 x 600 pixel image is scaled to be 5 inches wide, it would have a pixel density of 200 pixels per inch. If the same image is scaled to 10 inches wide, it would have a pixel density of only 100 pixels per inch. A higher pixel density results in a sharper image.

The amount of color information stored in an image, also known as color depth, impacts the amount of computer memory required for the picture. Color depth determines the range of colors the image can contain. Most images have either a color depth of 256 colors or 16.7 million colors. Simple charts, diagrams, cartoons, and clip art typically look fine with 256 colors, while photographs usually require 16.7 million colors.

Images with 16.7 million colors are also referred to as true color pictures or 24-bit color pictures.

A 4 x 6-inch photograph, which consists of over 2 million pixels, would require approximately 2MB of storage when using 256 colors. However, if true color is used, the picture size would increase significantly to 6.4MB. Thankfully, bitmap images can be compressed to reduce their size without noticeably distorting the image. Depending on the image's content, a 6MB picture may be compressed to 250KB or even less.

Vector

Apart from bitmap images, PowerPoint also supports the use of vector drawings. A vector drawing is a picture file that contains a precise definition of each shape within the image. These drawings are typically created using advanced drawing software like Adobe Illustrator.

PowerPoint is compatible with various popular vector drawing formats.

Inserting Pictures in Your Presentation

Are you ready for this? Whether you purchase PowerPoint separately or as part of Microsoft Office, you also gain access to an extensive online collection of clip art pictures that you can easily incorporate into your presentations. Additionally, you have the option to download images from the internet or utilize images already saved on your computer's hard drive.

However, it's important not to go overboard with pictures. Loading your presentation with multiple cliché clip art pictures on each slide will give it an unprofessional and amateurish appearance. Instead, exercising careful and selective use of pictures will yield more effective results.

From the web

If you wish to insert pictures into your presentation that you've downloaded from the web, follow these steps:

1. Ensure you are connected to the internet, as you won't be able to retrieve pictures from the web without an internet connection.

2. Move to the slide where you want to place the picture. If you want the same picture to appear on every slide, switch to Slide Master view.

3. Select the "Insert" tab on the Ribbon and click on "Pictures," followed by "Online Pictures." After a brief pause, the Online Pictures dialog box will appear.

4. Enter a keyword related to the picture you're looking for in the "Search Bing" text box, then press Enter. For example, if you're searching for pictures of William Shakespeare, type "Shakespeare" and press Enter.

PowerPoint will search Bing for the picture you specified and display thumbnail images of the results it finds.

5. Click on the picture you want to use, and then click "Insert." The picture will be inserted onto the current slide. When you insert a picture, a new tab called "Picture Format" will appear on the Ribbon. Additionally, the Design Ideas pane will appear, providing suggestions on how you can modify the appearance of the inserted picture.

Please be cautious when using Bing's image search, as some of the displayed images may be protected by copyright. Make sure you obtain permission from the copyright holder before using images found through Bing.

6. Feel free to drag and resize the picture as needed. For detailed instructions on moving, sizing, stretching, and cropping pictures, refer to the "Moving, Sizing, Stretching, and Cropping Pictures" section later in this chapter.

From your computer

If you already have an image file saved on your computer or in OneDrive that you want to add to your presentation in PowerPoint, follow these steps:

1. Go to the slide where you want to insert the picture.

2. Select the "Insert" tab on the Ribbon and click on "Pictures," followed by "This Device." The Insert Picture dialog box will appear.

3. Navigate through your computer's hard drive or OneDrive to locate the file you want to insert. Use the controls provided in the Insert Picture dialog box to search for the file effectively.

   If you have saved the picture in OneDrive, you can access it from there. Please note that OneDrive is available only if you use Office 365.

4. Click on the file you wish to insert, and then click "Insert."

   That's it! The picture will be inserted onto the slide as per your selection.

   Additionally, you can directly paste a picture into PowerPoint using the Clipboard. Anything you can copy to the Clipboard can be pasted into PowerPoint. For example, if you create a sketch using Windows Paint, you can copy it and then switch to PowerPoint to paste it. The image will be instantly inserted into your presentation.

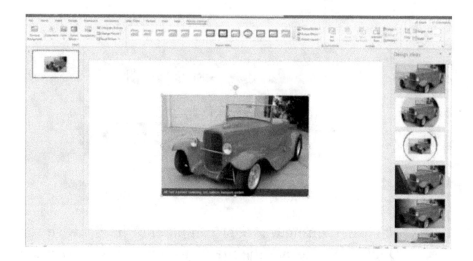

Moving, Sizing, Stretching, and Cropping Pictures

Because PowerPoint chooses an arbitrary position on the slide to insert pictures, you undoubtedly want to move the clip art to a more convenient location. You probably also want to change the size of the picture if it's too big or too small for your slide.

Follow these steps to force your inserted clip art into full compliance:

To adjust the positioning and size of a picture in PowerPoint, follow these steps:

1. **Click on the picture and drag it to the desired location on the slide.**

   You don't need to click precisely on the edges or lines of the picture, as clicking anywhere inside the picture allows you to drag it around.

2. To resize the picture, locate the eight handles (small squares or circles) surrounding the picture.

Click and drag any of these handles to adjust the size of the picture. When you click and drag one of the corner handles, the height and width of the picture change proportionally.

3. When you drag one of the edge handles (top, bottom, left, or right), you can change the size of the picture in only one dimension, which may distort the picture's appearance. When you resize a picture, its position on the slide may also change. Therefore, you may need to move the picture again after resizing it. However, if you hold down the Ctrl key while dragging a handle, the picture remains anchored at its center point during resizing, maintaining its position on the slide.

This can be useful if you want to resize the picture without adjusting its position.

Stretching a clip art picture by dragging one of the edge handles can significantly alter its appearance. For instance, you can stretch an object vertically to make it appear tall and thin, or horizontally to make it look short and wide.

In some cases, you may want to crop a picture to include only a specific part in your presentation. To do this:

Select the picture and click the "Crop" button located on the Picture Format tab of the Ribbon, in the Size group. The selection handles will change to crop marks.

Drag the crop marks around to cut off the unwanted areas of the picture.

Once you are satisfied with the cropped portion, press the Esc key to finalize the crop.

Note: It's important to know that cropping can be applied to bitmap images but not vector pictures.

If you later decide to undo the cropping and revert to the original picture, right-click on the picture, choose "Format Picture" from the menu, and click the "Reset" button.

These techniques allow you to adjust the positioning, size, and cropping of pictures in PowerPoint, giving you more control over their appearance in your presentation.

Adding Style to Your Pictures

PowerPoint offers the ability to enhance your pictures by applying stylistic features like borders, shadows, and reflections. By adding these effects, you can draw attention to your pictures and make them visually appealing.

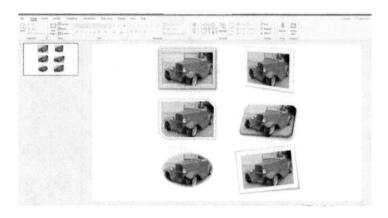

To apply a style effect to a picture in PowerPoint, follow these steps:

1. Select the picture you want to modify.

2. Go to the Picture Format tab on the Ribbon.

3. In the Picture Styles group, you will find various pre-defined picture styles to choose from.

4. Simply click on the desired picture style to apply it to the selected picture.

5. PowerPoint provides 28 predefined picture styles. Each style is a combination of three types of formatting options that can be individually applied to pictures: Shape, Border, and Effects. If desired, you can customize these formats individually using the following sections in PowerPoint.

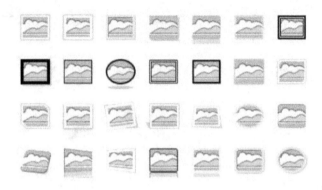

It's worth noting that if you utilize one of these predefined picture styles, the picture will automatically update if you later change the theme of the presentation. Hence, it is recommended to use one of the predefined styles whenever possible.

Applying a picture border

You can apply a border to a picture by selecting the Picture Format tab and clicking Picture Border in the Picture Styles group. This reveals the Picture Border menu, which lets you choose the border color, weight (the width of the border lines) and the pattern of dashes you want to use.

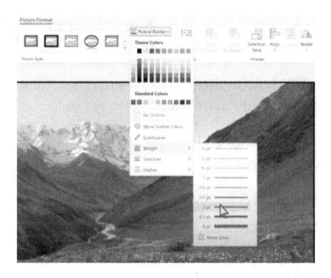

Note that if you've applied a shape to the picture, the border is applied to the shape.

Applying picture effects

In PowerPoint, you have the option to apply various effects to your pictures to enhance their appearance. These effects can be accessed through the Picture Effects button, located in the Picture Styles group on the Picture Format tab. When you click on this button, a menu will appear with the following options:

- **Shadow**: Applies a shadow effect to the picture. You can choose from predefined shadow effects or customize the shadow using a dialog box.

- **Reflection**: Creates a reflected image of the picture below the original picture, giving it a reflective look.

- **Glow**: Adds a glowing effect around the edges of the picture, making it stand out.

- **Soft Edges**: Softens the edges of the picture, giving it a smoother and more subtle appearance.

- **Bevel**: Creates a 3D beveled look for the picture, adding depth and dimension.

- **3D Rotation**: Allows you to rotate the picture in a way that creates a three-dimensional effect.

Applying the Artistic Effects

To use these effects, select the picture and go to the Picture Format tab. Click on the Picture Effects button and choose the desired effect from the menu.

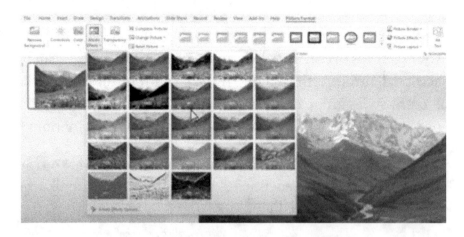

Additionally, PowerPoint offers the Artistic Effects command, which applies special filters to your pictures to give them an artistic appearance. When you click on the Artistic Effects button, you'll see a preview of how each effect will transform the selected image. Hovering the mouse over the effect will display its name. To apply an artistic effect, select the picture, go to the Picture Format tab, click on the Artistic Effects button, and select the desired effect.

It's important to note that the results of these effects may vary depending on the original picture, and it's recommended to experiment with them to see how they work.

Here's a list of the effects that are available:

- Blur

- Cement

- Chalk Sketch

- Crisscross Etching

- Cutout

- Film Grain

- Glass

- Glow Diffused

- Glow Edges

- Light Screen

- Line Drawing

- Marker

- Mosaic Bubbles

- Paint Brush

- Paint Strokes

- Pastels Smooth

- Pencil Grayscale

- Pencil Sketch

- Photocopy

- Plastic Wrap

- Texturizer

- Watercolor Sponge

Removing picture backgrounds

PowerPoint provides the feature to remove the background from a picture, allowing you to isolate the subject and remove any unwanted elements.

Here are the steps to remove the background from a picture:

1. Select the picture from which you want to remove the background.

2. Go to the Picture Format tab and click on the Remove Background button, located in the Adjust group.

   PowerPoint will attempt to determine the subject and background of the picture by creating a bounding rectangle around the subject and displaying the background in purple. The Background Removal tab will appear on the Ribbon.

3. PowerPoint's initial attempt may not be perfect, so you can use the Mark Areas to Keep and Mark Areas to Remove buttons to refine the background removal process.

   Use the Mark Areas to Keep button to include areas that PowerPoint has identified as the background but are actually part of the subject. Click or drag a line across the area to be included.

Use the Mark Areas to Remove button to mark areas that should be removed as part of the background. Click or draw a line within the area to be removed. If you make a mistake, press Ctrl+Z to undo your action or use the Delete Mark button to remove specific marks.

4. Repeat Step 4 as needed until you are satisfied with the background removal. You can mark multiple areas to keep or remove.

5. Once you have successfully removed the picture's background, click the Keep Changes button.

The slide will return to its normal view, and the background of the picture will be removed, isolating the subject.

Correcting Sharpness, Brightness, Contrast, and Color

Occasionally, despite your best attempts, your photographs simply don't turn out as you had hoped. They might be a little out of focus, too brilliant, too dark, faded, or contrasty. To enhance such images, there are several great programs available. Adobe Photoshop is one of the most popular and effective programs.

Nevertheless, PowerPoint has a number of capabilities that can do a lot of what Photoshop does. The Corrections command is one of them, and it can be useful when your photos need a little careful care and attention. You can change the sharpness, brightness, and contrast of a picture with this command, which can be found in the Adjust section of the Picture Format tab.

Click the Corrections button, then select one of the pre-set alternatives from the list of available options to alter the sharpness, brightness, or contrast of a photograph. To access the Picture Corrections controls in the task pane to the right of the slide. Select the Picture Correction Options command from the bottom of the Corrections menu. To give this image a distinct appearance, I changed the sharpness, brightness, and contrast.

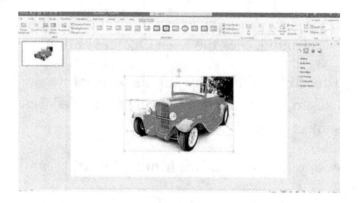

You can change the color of your images using the Color button found in the Picture Format tab's Adjust section. The following elements of a picture's color can be changed:

- **Color Saturation:** The picture's overall level of color

- **Tonal Colors:** The general "warmth" of the color in the image

- **Recolor:** The dominant hue that may be seen in the image

Click the Color button on the Picture Format tab and pick an option from the list of pre-set options to alter the color of an image. Alternatively, select the Picture Color Options option from the Color menu's bottom.

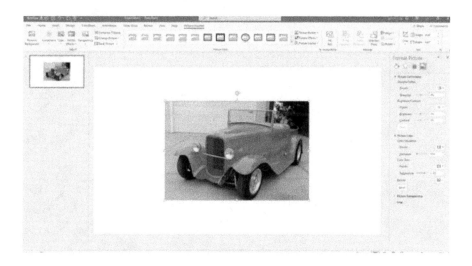